Remembering
Boston

Timothy Orwig

TURNER
PUBLISHING COMPANY

In 1911, people gather in front of the Boston Public Library in Copley Square to inaugurate Lemeuel Murlin as the new president of Boston University. Boston University was established in 1869 with a mission to educate students without regard to race, sex, or creed. It began on Beacon Hill before moving to quarters next to the library.

Remembering
Boston

Turner Publishing Company
www.turnerpublishing.com

Remembering Boston

Copyright © 2010 Turner Publishing Company

Library of Congress Control Number: 2010902291

ISBN: 978-1-59652-617-4

Printed in the United States of America

ISBN 978-1-68336-812-0 (pbk.)

CONTENTS

ACKNOWLEDGMENTS.. VII

PREFACE VIII

NINETEENTH-CENTURY BOSTON 1
    (1850s–1899)

BOSTON IN THE NEW CENTURY... 33
    (1900–1919)

BOSTON BETWEEN THE WARS... 71
    (1920–1939)

WAR, RECOVERY, AND BOSTON AT A CROSSROADS..117
    (1940–1950s)

NOTES ON THE PHOTOGRAPHS 131

The Boston and Lowell Railroad Station on Causeway Street, shown here upon its completion in 1871, was a grand French Renaissance structure. Designed by Levi Newcomb and Son, its concourse was paneled with oak and floored in marble. It was demolished in 1927.

ACKNOWLEDGMENTS

This volume, *Remembering Boston,* is the result of the cooperation and efforts of many individuals and organizations. It is with great thanks that we acknowledge the following for their generous support:

Boston Public Library
City of Boston Archives

We would also like to thank the following individuals
for their valuable contributions and assistance in making this work possible:

Roger Reed
Aaron Schmidt, Boston Public Library Print Department
Kristen Swett, City of Boston Archives

PREFACE

Boston has thousands of historic photographs that reside in archives, both locally and nationally. This book began with the observation that, while those photographs are of great interest to many, they are not easily accessible. During a time when Boston is looking ahead and evaluating its future course, many people are asking, How do we treat the past? These decisions affect every aspect of the city—architecture, public spaces, commerce, infrastructure—and these, in turn, affect the way that people live their lives. This book seeks to provide easy access to a valuable, objective look into the history of Boston.

The power of photographs is that they are less subjective than words in their treatment of history. Although the photographer can make subjective decisions regarding subject matter and how to capture and present it, photographs seldom interpret the past to the extent textual histories can. For this reason, photography is uniquely positioned to offer an original, untainted look at the past, allowing the viewer to learn for himself what the world was like a century or more ago.

This project represents countless hours of review and research. The researchers and writer have reviewed thousands of photographs in numerous archives. We greatly appreciate the generous assistance of the individuals and organizations listed in the acknowledgments of this work, without whom this project could not have been completed.

The goal in publishing this work is to provide broader access to this set of extraordinary photographs that seek to inspire, provide perspective, and evoke insight that might assist people who are responsible for determining Boston's future. In addition, the book seeks to preserve the past with adequate respect and reverence.

With the exception of touching up imperfections that have accrued with the passage of time and cropping where necessary, no changes have been made. The focus and clarity of many images are limited to the technology and the ability of the photographer at the time they were recorded.

The work is divided into eras. Beginning with some of the earliest known photographs of Boston, the first section records photographs from before the Civil War through the end of the nineteenth century. The second section spans the beginning of the twentieth century up to the start of Prohibition. Section Three moves from the twenties to the close of the Great Depression era. The last section takes a brief look at the World War II and postwar eras.

In each of these sections we have made an effort to capture various aspects of life through our selection of photographs. People, commerce, transportation, infrastructure, religious institutions, and educational institutions have been included to provide a broad perspective.

We encourage readers to reflect as they go walking in Boston, strolling through the city, its parks, and its neighborhoods. It is the publisher's hope that in utilizing this work, longtime residents will learn something new and that new residents will gain a perspective on where Boston has been, so that each can contribute to its future.

—*Todd Bottorff, Publisher*

The Boston and Providence
Railroad Station opened in Park
Square in 1872. Designed by
Peabody and Stearns, it was the
world's longest station at 850 feet.
Abandoned after South Station
opened in 1900, the station
was eventually replaced with
the Statler Building (Park Plaza
Hotel).

Nineteenth-century Boston

(1850–1899)

The Cathedral of the Holy Cross, on Franklin Street, was designed by architect Charles Bulfinch and built 1800–1803. Bulfinch drew up the plans as a gift for his friend Bishop John Cheverus, and President John Adams and others subscribed to build Boston's first Roman Catholic cathedral. This view dates to circa 1850. The building was demolished in 1862.

This photograph from circa 1855 shows the Marine and Eagle (at right) hotels. They stood at the corner of Lewis and Fulton streets in the North End, near Lewis Wharf, convenient to sailors and travelers.

On September 17, 1856, spectators crowd the ledges and rooftops on Court Street for a parade inaugurating the statue of Benjamin Franklin. Sculptor Richard Greenough's monument to Boston's favorite son stands in front of Old City Hall on neighboring School Street.

India and Central wharves are shown in 1857 crowded with ships. They were built out into the harbor between 1803 and 1816. The New England Aquarium was built on Central Wharf in 1969.

The National Theatre began in 1831 in a building on Traverse Street, in the Bulfinch Triangle. The building was destroyed by fire. This 1860 image shows its Italianate-style replacement, fronting on Portland Street, which opened in 1852.

Members of the Torrent Six company pose in front of their Roxbury fire station, about 1865. Eustis Street Fire Station, designed by local architect John Roulestone Hall and built in 1859, still anchors this historic district near Dudley Station.

This 1865 view of Washington Street shows the Old South Meeting House, Boston's second-oldest church, built by Joshua Blanchard in 1729. The congregation included Samuel Adams, Benjamin Franklin, and Phyllis Wheatley, and the church hosted the debates that led to the Boston Tea Party.

This 1869 view shows the Old Masonic Temple (1832), designed by Isaiah Rogers, at Tremont Street and Temple Place, which stood next to St. Paul's (Episcopal) Cathedral. Bronson Alcott, father of Louisa May Alcott, ran a school on the second floor of this Gothic granite building.

Quincy Market, designed by Alexander Parris and completed in 1826, was named after Josiah Quincy, the mayor who demolished a maze of wharves and alleys for its construction. In 1870, as shown here, it held agricultural businesses such as Ames Plow Company, and butchers hung carcasses in the halls where tourists shop today.

Established in 1800, the Charlestown Navy Yard built and repaired hundreds of ships, such as the USS *Kearsarge,* shown here in 1870. The wharves of the North End can be seen across the Charles River.

The Rogers Building (built 1863-65) on Boylston Street, shown in the 1870s, was designed by William Gibbons Preston. The Massachusetts Institute of Technology held its first classes here in 1875, but moved to a new campus in Cambridge in 1913. The building was demolished in 1939.

Fort Hill was an 80-foot hill overlooking the harbor and home to a colonial fort. The fort was replaced with a fashionable neighborhood around a circular square, but gradually the grand houses became tenements. The city leveled Fort Hill in 1870, loading it by steam shovel into horse-drawn tipcarts and railcars, which dumped the earth and rock into the harbor below. Today the Financial District skyscrapers reach higher than the hill they replaced.

Nothing remained of Franklin Street after the fire of November 9, 1872. Bostonians took comfort, though, in stories of the brave battle which saved the Old South Meeting House, whose spire stands a block away over the ruins in the background.

Pearl Street was also leveled in the Great Fire of 1872, which consumed 776 buildings crowded into 60 acres. The fire began in the basement of a hoop-skirt factory at Summer and Kingston streets.

Charlestown celebrated the centennial of the Battle of Bunker Hill on June 17, 1875, with a triumphal arch at City Square. Although the Colonial defenders lost that battle (which actually took place on Breed's Hill), Boston celebrated their fierce resistance.

Once widely known throughout New England, Ferdinand's Blue Store began in this building (photographed around 1880) at the southeast corner of Washington and Warren streets in Roxbury. By 1899, the growing store had replaced this building with a 5-story brick and limestone commercial palace, followed by an 8-story addition.

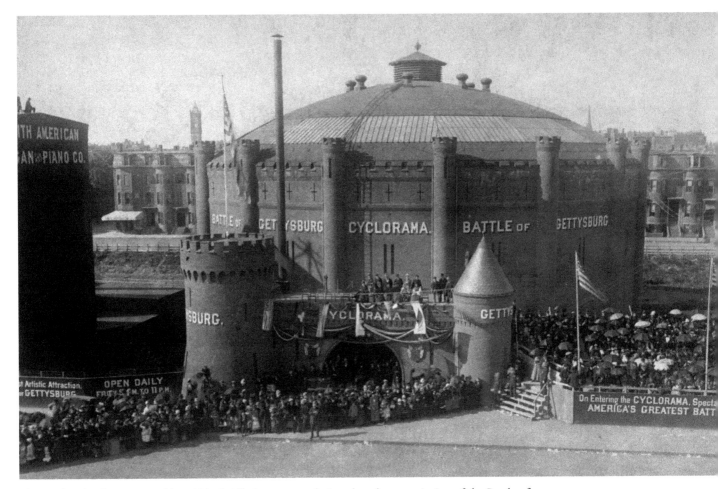

Shown shortly after it opened in 1884, the Cyclorama was designed to show a painting of the Battle of Gettysburg, 50 feet high by 400 feet long, in a full circle. Despite later additions, the building remains a landmark in the South End, part of the Boston Center for the Arts.

Taken about 1885, this photograph shows the Old State House (1712), at the head of State Street. The Old State House was restored in 1881, after Bostonians rallied to prevent Chicago from buying and moving it.

This early photograph shows the south side of the corner of Boylston and Tremont streets, with the home of John Quincy Adams (at left) and the Hotel Pelham (at right; 1857), the first apartment house in eastern America. They were eventually replaced with the Hotel Touraine (1897) and the Little Building (1916).

In 1809, John Quincy Adams laid the cornerstone for the Boylston Hall and Market on Boylston Street, shown here shortly before its 1888 demolition. All that survived of this building designed by Charles Bulfinch was the clock and cupola, which were incorporated into a church in Arlington, Massachusetts.

Scollay Square Station, with its four-sided clock and 1898 date block, shows Boston's civic pride in its subway system. This station and most of the surrounding buildings were leveled in the 1960s for Government Center.

Washington Street was once the only connection between the mainland and the colonial city of Boston on the Shawmut peninsula. Shown here in the 1890s, it was Boston's "Main Street," its stone block surface bisected by streetcar tracks.

This image shows a Chinese funeral on Harrison Avenue circa 1890. Chinese immigrants began opening businesses along Harrison in 1875; by 1890 Boston's Chinatown extended from Kneeland to Essex streets.

The Harvard College Medical School, founded in Cambridge in 1782 and moved to Boston in 1810, erected this building (designed by Ware and Van Brunt) on Boylston Street in 1881. After the medical school moved to the Longwood neighborhood, Boston University used the building for classes. The Boston Public Library built a large addition on the site in 1971.

Seen here circa 1890, Copley Square is dominated by the Romanesque-revival tower of Trinity Church (1872-77), designed by H. H. Richardson (shown from the rear, at the corner of Clarendon and St. James). To the right of the church is its attached cloister and parish house; to the left, across Copley Square, is the Boston Public Library.

Faneuil Hall, shown here in the 1890s, with Quincy Market to the right. A gift to the city by Peter Faneuil in 1740, Faneuil Hall was designed by painter John Smibert. In 1804, Charles Bulfinch enlarged the building, doubling its width, adding a third story, and moving its cupola to the harbor end.

Following in the tradition of colonial militias, the Third Battalion, Boston School Regiment, of Boston Latin School poses on the Boston Common in 1892. A crowd has gathered at the base of the Soldiers and Sailors Monument in the background to witness the battalion's annual review.

Narrow, winding Salem Street in the North End was home to successive waves of Irish, Jewish, and Italian immigrants. This 1893 photograph shows a laundry at Prince Street, where Salem begins a steep climb toward Old North Church (1723).

A view from August 1897 shows the training trolley entering the subway from Boylston Street, at the Public Garden. Gradually, Boston expanded its subway system, but most trains outside downtown still run on surface tracks.

Boston opened the nation's first subway on September 1, 1897, to alleviate congestion on its crowded streets. This photograph shows conductors in training, crowded into a trolley at a bend near Park Street Station.

This view shows Copley Square from the roof of the Boston Public Library. Until 1969, Huntington Avenue cut diagonally across the square to join Boylston Street, preventing any substantial park development. The ivy-covered church to the extreme left, Second (Unitarian) Church, was replaced with an office building in 1914.

Boston in the New Century

(1900–1919)

Though this photograph is thought to date to circa 1900, the Union Oyster House is almost timeless. It was built circa 1713-17 as the Capen House. An early anti-British newspaper, the *Massachusetts Spy,* was published upstairs in 1771. Opened downstairs in 1826, the Union Oyster House is the oldest continuously operating restaurant in the nation.

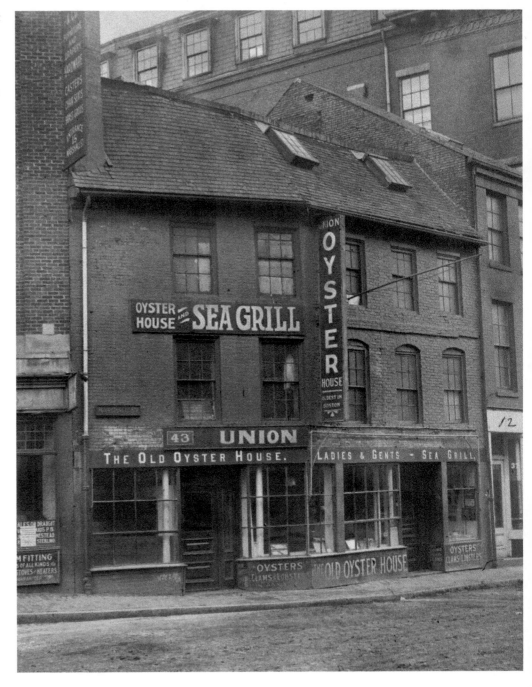

St. Peter's, on Meeting House Hill (shown ca. 1900), is the oldest and largest Roman Catholic church in Dorchester. Designed by Patrick Keeley and built from puddingstone quarried on its Bowdoin Street site, the building was begun in 1872. The tower and finials were finished in 1891.

Park Square circa 1900, looking straight down Columbus Street, with the tower of the Boston and Providence Railroad Station to the right. At left middle is the Thomas Ball statue *Emancipation Group* (1875).

Boston began the first postal service in the colonies in 1639, with Richard Fairbanks' Boston tavern designated the first post office. The massive post office building to the left, in Post Office Square (shown here ca. 1906), is one of its successors, built in 1869. The sharp-edged Delta Building, to the right, was replaced in 1929.

Merchant's Row (shown here ca. 1900) was the street which bisected Faneuil Hall and Quincy Market. The buildings of Joseph Breck and Sons, which stood at 47-54 North Market Street, show how merchants could turn every surface of a building into advertising space.

Castle Square Theatre (shown here ca. 1900) was on Tremont Street in the South End. Built in 1888 as a cyclorama to display a painting of the Battle of Bunker Hill, the theater was encased in a 500-room hotel in 1894. Besides opera and theater (Alfred Lunt was a member of its stock company), Castle Square hosted movies (beginning in 1917). Anchor of an immigrant neighborhood, the building was demolished in 1933.

Just a block long, Park Street defines the eastern edge of the Boston Common and provides a dramatic view (ca. 1900) of the Massachusetts State House on Beacon Street. Its beginning has been marked since 1810 by the elegantly rounded front and telescoping spire of the Park Street Church (to the right), which graces Tremont Street.

Temple Place in 1900, seen from the Common at Tremont Street. Named after Boston's first Masonic Temple, which stood on the left, the street changed from residential to business uses during the nineteenth century.

Little distinguishes the red-brick buildings of the North Slope of Beacon Hill (foreground) from those of the West End (beyond) in this view from circa 1900, while the Bunker Hill monument marks Charlestown in the distance, across the Charles River. The church tower to the right belongs to the Old West Church (1806, Asher Benjamin, architect) on Cambridge Street, which marked the line between the neighborhoods.

This 1901 photograph reveals only a portion of the massive Union Station (1894) by Shepley, Rutan, and Coolidge. Built between the old Lowell and Fitchburg stations, it linked them into a grand facade along Causeway Street. The entire complex was leveled in 1927, replaced by North Station and the Boston Garden.

Shepley, Rutan, and Coolidge's South Station (1899) provides a suitable backdrop for a procession through Dewey Square honoring Vice-president Theodore Roosevelt on April 29, 1901. In the carriage (at center) with Roosevelt, is George Draper, president of the Home Market Club, the group Roosevelt addressed the next evening. Roosevelt became president of the United States that September, when President McKinley was assassinated.

At nine-thirty in the morning on June 25, 1903, Joseph Hooker Wood loosened a silk ribbon and unveiled the statue of his grand-uncle, General "Fighting Joe" Hooker. Though best known for his defeat at Chancellorsville, Hooker served bravely throughout the Civil War. The bronze statue of Hooker was sculptured by Daniel Chester French and the horse by Edward C. Potter.

The 1902 Boston visit of Prince Heinrich of Prussia, brother of Emperor Wilhelm II, included an honorary doctorate from Harvard and a visit to the State House on March 6. The latter was comic. Both houses of the legislature had gathered for a state address, but no one had actually invited Prince Henry to speak. After awkward silence, the puzzled prince sat down. Governor Winthrop Crane quickly escorted him back to his carriage.

On August 9, 1904, a horse-drawn steam fire engine gallops by an open electric trolley on Washington Street. In the background, on either side of Milk Street, are the Old South Meeting House (1729), and, covered with bunting, the Boston Transcript building. All the buildings this side of Milk Street were built after the Great Fire of 1872.

Shown here circa 1905 is the shop of Lally Brothers, Blacksmiths and Wheelwrights, in the industrial Fort Point Channel neighborhood. A cart for Frank Jones Brewing Company is up on blocks for repairs. In 1893, more than 500 carriage workers went on strike against Lally Brothers and other Boston firms, successfully securing a 9-hour workday.

Third baseman Jimmy Collins jumps for the ball in a posed action shot, circa 1905. Collins began his major league career with the Boston Beaneaters in 1895. He joined the Boston Americans as player-manager when they formed in 1901, and led them to the 1903 World Championship. He left for the Philadelphia Athletics in 1907, the year the Americans became the Boston Red Sox.

The ferry *Governor Russell* plies the waters in June 1905, carrying passengers and horse carts across the Boston Harbor. The *Governor Russell* was a propeller ferryboat built by William McKee in 1899, on the same lines as his *Noddle Island,* which set a record 14 miles per hour when first launched.

The Sherwin Williams Company (which adopted the "Cover the Earth" logo in 1906) had a distribution center on Purchase Street. Beginning in 1906 its New England employees gathered at Canobie Lake Park in New Hampshire for annual company outings.

This 1907 photograph shows Spring Street and Poplar Street in the West End. Early in the 1800s the West End had been a fashionable upper-class neighborhood. A century later, it was a remarkable working-class neighborhood of African-Americans, immigrants from Ireland, Poland, and Italy, and Jews from the Pale of Russia.

Automobiles are gradually displacing horse-drawn vehicles amid the electric trolleys on Washington Street on August 19, 1908. Houston and Henderson Company, a dry-goods store at Temple Place, used the advertising slogan "the Busiest Corner on Boston's Busiest Street."

Paul Revere's House, on North Square in the North End (shown here in 1909), is the oldest surviving building in downtown Boston. Built about 1680, it was already ninety years old when Paul Revere moved in (1770). On the night of April 18, 1775, Revere left this house and rode to Lexington to warn Samuel Adams and John Hancock that British troops were coming to arrest them, a ride later immortalized by poet Henry Wadsworth Longfellow.

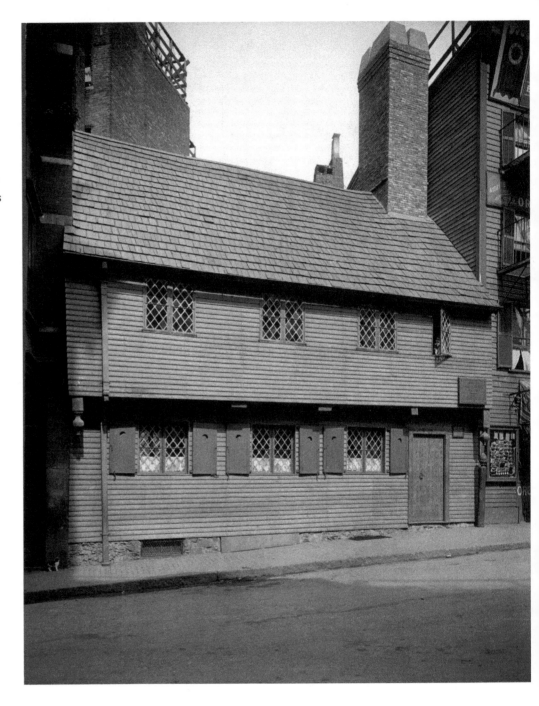

Tourists are a long-standing Boston tradition. This photograph from circa 1910 shows the Boston Palace Car, with its driver and bullhorn-wielding guide. The sign on the side of the open car advertises that the tour "starts opposite Hotel Touraine at 10-2-4."

The third Suffolk County Court House (1896; designed by George A. Clough) obliterated half of Pemberton Square, an 1830s park-centered neighborhood much like Louisburg Square on Beacon Hill. This view shows the courthouse before a tall mansard roof was added in 1906-9.

The Hemenway Building (1883, center) by Bradlee, Winslow, and Wetherell, in view here circa 1910, is unremarkable except for its whimsical 6th-floor corner oriel window. Most of the rest of the surrounding Scollay Square, including the statue of Governor John Winthrop, was removed in the 1960s for Government Center.

Automobiles had not displaced horse travel completely by 1910, in evidence in this view of sleighs parading along Beacon Street.

This picture shows the West End in 1910. This is the corner of Chambers and Spring streets, looking toward Leverett Street. The West End, sandwiched between Beacon Hill and the Bulfinch Triangle, held as many as 7,000 inhabitants.

Spectators fill Harvard Stadium in 1914 for "the Game," the annual November competition between the Harvard Crimson and the Yale Bulldogs. The rivalry began in 1875. Harvard's "flying wedge" of 1892 caused both injuries on the Yale team and early attention to regularizing rules. Ivy League football made popular such college traditions as pennants, mascots, fight songs, and pranking.

This 1915 aerial shot shows Harvard Stadium, in Boston's Allston neighborhood. Designed by McKim, Mead, and White and opened in 1903, the first permanent college stadium was also a pioneering use of reinforced concrete. The horseshoe shape evoked Greek amphitheaters and Roman stadia.

This photograph shows granite works behind the State House, presumably part of the extension of the State House. The Massachusetts State House was significantly expanded from 1914 to 1917, with two large wings (designed by Chapman, Sturgis, and Andrews) bracketing the original 1795-97 building.

Most Bostonians would immediately recognize Symphony Hall (1900; McKim, Mead, and White), to the left in this 1916 photograph. Receding into the distance along Westland Avenue is the castle-like form of the less-known Boston Storage Warehouse, reduced to a parking lot in 1955.

Bowdoin Square Baptist Church (1840), designed by Richard Bond, in view here circa 1915. The church was built of brick, with an unhammered granite front that included a 110-foot Gothic tower. It was razed for the New England Telephone Building (1930).

The United States remained neutral for almost three years before entering the First World War in April 1917. As part of the mobilization, the Massachusetts State Militia came under federal control. This image, dated July 28, 1917, shows the first muster of the Massachusetts militia under federal orders, marching up Beacon Street and down Park Street.

Despite its timeless air, the Massachusetts State House has gone through many changes, including two rear extensions in the 1800s, and these new marble wings, completed in 1917. The red-brick center section, known as the Bulfinch front (after its architect Charles Bulfinch), survived an 1890s effort to replace it. Long painted yellow, it was painted white in 1918 to match the marble wings. The paint was finally removed in 1928.

In 1918, children stricken with infantile paralysis (poliomyelitis) were transferred to a clinic by the Children's Ambulance Service. A rare condition until the 1890s, polio was feared as a mysterious crippler of children throughout the first half of the century, until the Salk and Sabin vaccines were devised in the 1950s and 1960s.

The circular pile of debris just in front of the light-colored warehouse is all that remains of the tank that held more than two million gallons of molasses. Used as a sweetener, molasses was also an ingredient in alcohol and munitions. Rather than repair the leaks in the tank, the company had painted it brown to hide them. It initially blamed anarchists for the disaster.

Copley Square as it appeared in 1919, from the tower of Trinity Church (its roof is visible at lower-left). Across Boylston Street, to the right of the Boston Public Library, rises the tower of the New Old South Church (1874-75). All of Copley Square is built on unstable fill. The 246-foot tower of this Congregational church began tilting, and had to be dismantled in 1931. By 1940, a shorter—but stable—tower rose in its place.

From the vantage point of the Boston Wharf buildings, this photograph shows downtown Boston in 1919, just beyond the Northern Avenue Bridge over the Fort Point Channel. The single skyscraper is the tower of the Custom House. Completed in 1915, this tower circumvented downtown Boston's 125-foot height restriction because it was federally owned.

Boston Between the Wars

(1920–1939)

On May 27, 1921, Boston kids try out a new "sprinkling device" for keeping cool in the summer. On the sidewalk behind them, social classes are clearly delineated, as those in ties and hats keep a safe distance from the splashing, while workmen in cloth caps enjoy the revelry.

Trotters at Readville Park, circa 1920. Located in the Hyde Park neighborhood of Boston on the Dedham town line, Readville began as a Union training camp during the Civil War, and then a county fairgrounds. The mile-long Readville Trotting Park that opened there in 1896 became the premier site for harness racing in New England through the 1920s.

On a tour of Boston, General John J. Pershing meets with Governor Calvin Coolidge outside the Massachusetts State House on February 25, 1920. Hero of the Spanish-American War and campaigns in Mexico and the Philippines, Pershing served as the leader of U.S. forces in Europe in the First World War. Coolidge, who had gained national attention by breaking a Boston police strike in 1919, became vice-president in 1921 and president in 1923.

This view from circa 1920 looks from the top of the Ames Building toward old Dock Square, and the North End beyond. To the right is Faneuil Hall. The neighborhood in the foreground disappeared for the Boston City Hall and Government Center, and the neighborhood beyond for the Central Artery elevated highway.

Looking down Commonwealth Avenue at the Hotel Somerset, on September 6, 1920. Designed by architect Arthur Bowditch in 1897, it was one of several apartment buildings along the Charlesgate Fens that attracted wealthy Social-Register residents to the western Back Bay in the 1920s.

Charles Ponzi on his way to court, August 1920. An Italian immigrant, Ponzi hit upon a scheme of buying and selling international postal reply coupons and made a fortune in currency trading, mostly from gullible investors. Ponzi pled guilty to mail fraud in November 1920, and Bostonians lost millions of dollars. "Ponzi scheme" remains a term to describe a clever investment fraud.

In the winter of 1920, workers unload fish at a South Boston pier. Originally a peninsula off Dorchester, South Boston was annexed to Boston in 1804. Its pastures were overlaid with a regular grid of streets. South Boston became an industrial engine for Boston, with foundries, machine shops, refineries, and shipyards employing a large immigrant workforce.

Firemen pose with their fire engine in East Boston, possibly Saratoga Street, circa 1920. With its shipyards, warehouses, and wharves, East Boston attracted waves of workers from many nations, including Ireland, Canada, Italy, Greece, and Portugal. By 1905, the influx of Russian and Eastern European Jews made East Boston the largest Jewish community on the East Coast.

The Massachusetts Society for the Prevention of Cruelty to Animals sponsored several fountains for watering horses in downtown Boston (shown here in 1922). Founded by Boston lawyer George Angell in 1868, the MSPCA sparked a national movement, which led to laws protecting animals from unnecessary abuse and established animal shelters and hospitals.

This Back Bay view, looking down Stuart Street from Dartmouth Street, shows the first of the three John Hancock buildings in 1922, the year it was completed. Designed by Parker, Thomas, and Rice, the building still stands, although a subsequent addition stacked four more floors atop the original building, encasing its distinctive tower.

This aerial view of 1925 Boston shows Fan Pier to the lower right, with the Northern Avenue Bridge over the Fort Point Channel to the left. The single substantial tower downtown is the Custom House. Most of the land along the Boston Harbor has a complex history of centuries of dock construction, followed by harbor filling and building construction; today the original shoreline is often buried several blocks inland.

Rush hour at Quincy Market circa 1925, as a line of horse-drawn wagons, most carrying fresh produce for the market, threads past parked automobiles.

This image from October 1925 shows Stuart Street, in Boston's Theater District, looking west from Washington Street toward Tremont. The district's oldest restaurant is on the right at 31–39 Stuart Street (its clock visible just below the "Hardware" sign). Jacob Wirth's, a German brew pub, opened in this block in 1868, moved to a bowfront Greek Revival house across the street in 1878, and expanded into its neighboring bowfront in 1891.

Perhaps no other landmark in Boston has been photographed as frequently as the Quincy Market. This 1926 view shows—through the billboards—the dome of Quincy Market and the cupola of Faneuil Hall. Atop the cupola is the famed grasshopper weathervane designed by Deacon Shem Drowne and erected above Faneuil Hall in 1742.

This March 1927 photograph shows busy Tremont Street from the Little Building on Boylston Street. On the left is the Boylston Street T Station, at the edge of the Boston Common. The Little Building (1916) was designed by Blackall, Clapp, and Whittemore, an architectural firm responsible for a number of theaters in the surrounding district.

Governor Alvan T. Fuller presents Amelia Earhart with a bouquet of roses at the Massachusetts State House in July 1928. The month before, Earhart had been the first woman to copilot a transatlantic flight, followed by the second solo transatlantic flight in 1932. In 1937, Earhart attempted to be the first woman to fly around the world, but disappeared over the South Pacific.

Boston Bruins General Manager Art Ross looks on as the team goalie shows a boy how to protect
the net at the Boston Garden in 1929. The Boston Bruins hockey team debuted in 1924 and played
its first season at the new Boston Garden in 1928-29. The city built the Boston Garden stadium on
Causeway Street, above its new North Station.

Haymarket Square on September 22, 1929, with the Custom House Tower and the cupola of Faneuil Hall (center) visible down the intersecting streets. This photograph was taken from the vantage point of the Haymarket Square Relief Hospital (1900), an emergency center designed to quickly treat those injured in industrial accidents: Boston's first ambulance station.

The *Spirit of St. Louis* in Boston, in 1927, probably July 22 or 23. On May 20, 1927, Charles Lindbergh became the first man to fly nonstop across the Atlantic in a fixed-wing aircraft, flying from New York to Paris and collecting a $25,000 prize. Lindbergh called his plane *Spirit of St. Louis* after city leaders there financed its purchase. Today the plane is in the Smithsonian National Air and Space Museum in Washington, D.C.

This view in May 1929 shows the Custom House Tower from the Boston waterfront, with the Eastern Packet Pier in the foreground.

The first regularly scheduled passenger plane to run between Boston and New York left Boston (later Logan) Airport on April 14, 1927. The U.S. Army completed the airfield (for military flights) in 1923 on tidal flats on the south edge of East Boston. In 1925, the Boston Aircraft Corporation completed the first commercial hangar, and in 1927 Colonial Air Transport (later American Airlines) began passenger service.

North Street in the North End (viewed from Fleet Street) is decorated for a feast day celebration on June 23, 1929. First organized by local Italian social clubs in the 1890s, feast day celebrations include public processions. Club members carry shrines with statues of their patron saints, and celebrants pin cash donations to ribbons hanging from the shrines.

The United Shoe Machinery building, designed by Parker, Thomas, and Rice, shown during construction (ca. 1929). With its 34-story tower, elegant setbacks, tiled cap, and Art Deco styling, the building helped introduce the modern skyscraper to a hesitant, tradition-bound Boston.

The Hotel Kensington was known for its stone lions, including this one looking over Copley Square, circa 1930. Behind the lion, at left, is the tower of the New Old South Church. To the right is the Beaux Arts–style Boston Public Library, with Trinity Church (Episcopal) and its parish house across Copley Square.

Five friends wave from atop a fence in one of Boston's residential neighborhoods.

"Pushcart rush at Clinton Street in the Market District, 3 p.m." Pushcarts, shown here circa 1930, were a way for poor immigrants to start careers in Boston. Several wealthy Boston merchants, such as bookseller and publisher Thomas O. H. P. Burnham, began careers with a Quincy Market pushcart.

Bathing in the Frog Pond, on the Boston Common, circa 1930. The last of three original ponds for watering cattle on the Boston Common, the Frog Pond was remade as a public fountain in 1848 to celebrate the opening of the Cochituate reservoir. Today it is popular year-round, for bathing, ice-skating, or as a reflecting pool, depending on the season.

City Hospital in the South End, from Worcester Square, circa 1930. Gridley J. F. Bryant designed
Boston City Hospital (1862-64) so that its main pavilion was framed by Worcester Square, across
Harrison Avenue. Laid out by the city in 1851 and developed a decade later, Worcester Square is
characterized by its uniform rows of bowfront townhouses surrounding a long, narrow square.

A Roxbury theater used its sound truck to try to slow a run on neighborhood banks in December 1931. The Federal National Bank and the Boston Continental Bank, like hundreds of others around the nation, were threatened with insolvency when a number of patrons withdrew their money at the same time.

Guay's Bakery, shown here apparently after a fire, was at 786 Adams Street in Dorchester, circa 1930, with Jos. Grevis Hardware to the right. Dorchester, founded a month before Boston in 1630, remained a country town almost until annexed by Boston in 1870. Adams Street was one of its earliest roads, and business centers formed around intersections like this one.

A jumble of automobiles, horse carts, and pushcarts crowds the portico of Quincy Market, circa 1930. This block has been Boston's market district for nearly four centuries, beginning as the Town Dock in 1633. In 1740, the dock was replaced by Faneuil Hall, with Quincy Market added in 1826.

A blizzard lends an air of romance to Scollay Square, circa 1930. Visible between the buildings at right is the famous steaming teakettle sign. Erected in 1873 by the Oriental Tea Company, the sign was a fixture of Scollay Square, moving several times before coming to rest (around 1960) on the Sears Block. Historic preservationists helped save the Sears Block and its sign during the Government Center redevelopment of the 1960s.

On June 3, 1931, the USS *Constitution* unfurls its sails at the Charlestown Navy Yard. The oldest commissioned vessel in the U.S. Navy, the frigate was designed by Joshua Humphrey and built in 1794-97 at Hartt's Shipyard in Boston. "Old Ironsides" fought pirates on the Barbary Coast and the British during the War of 1812. Restored in 1925, she began a tour of 90 port cities in 1931.

In May of 1932, members of the Women's Naval Reserve ride a Swan Boat at the Public Garden. Devised in 1877 by Robert Paget, the Swan Boat is a catamaran fitted with a paddlewheel. It is powered by a bicycle mechanism operated by its captain, who sits in the swan. The pond at the center of the Public Garden was modeled after the Serpentine in London's Hyde Park.

Arthur Stanek of Boston's West Roxbury neighborhood campaigned against Prohibition in 1932 at
the Massachusetts State House. The 18th Amendment to the Constitution began Prohibition in 1920
by outlawing the manufacture, transport, and sale of alcoholic beverages in the United States. Late in
1933, the 21st Amendment repealed Prohibition.

Auto racing began at Readville Race Track in 1903 and had displaced horse racing by the late 1920s. This view, from July 1932, shows pit crews working on their vehicles before the race. In the early 1930s, the track's owners used fill from the excavation of the Sumner Tunnel to build and bank the track for automobiles. Races continued through 1937.

Mayor James Michael Curley welcomed Budweiser back to Boston in 1933. The Blaine Act allowed the sale of 3.2 percent beer on April 7. Bostonians celebrated across the city. Downtown cafes filled with patrons, while society matrons, gentlemen in derby hats, and Harvard students lined up at the S. S. Pierce and Company warehouse in Brookline to buy crates of beer.

Franklin Delano Roosevelt speaks in Boston from his automobile, likely in late October 1932, during his campaign for the presidency. FDR had many Boston connections, having graduated from Groton School (in Groton, Massachusetts) and Harvard. Despite being partly paralyzed in 1921, Roosevelt campaigned successfully for governor of New York (1928-32) and president (1933-45).

Horse racing at Suffolk Downs in 1935, the year it opened. Massachusetts legalized pari-mutuel betting in 1935, and Suffolk Downs was built in 62 days upon former mudflats in East Boston. On July 10, 1935, 35,000 spectators turned out for the first race. Seabiscuit raced here in 1937, and the Beatles played their last Boston concert here in 1966.

Shown about 1935, the *Nantasket* (built ca. 1902) sailed regularly from the Atlantic Avenue piers south to Connecticut. Behind it is the Eastern Steamship Line's *Belfast* (built in 1909 at the Bath Iron Works in Maine), which sailed regularly between Boston and Bangor, Maine. The Eastern Steamship Line, formed in 1901 from the merger of several New England lines, offered regular service along the coast until 1941.

A native of West Medford, Massachusetts, Johnny Kelley won the Boston Athletic Association Marathon on April 19, 1935. Kelley also won the Boston Marathon in 1945 and placed second 7 times, competing a record 61 times before his death in 2004. The oldest (1897) and most revered marathon in the United States, the Boston Marathon was inspired by the Athens Olympics of 1896.

Boston's market district, viewed on a snowy January day in 1936 from the Ames Building. Automobiles had already begun to affect Boston: the narrow downtown streets near Faneuil Hall have been straightened or widened, and other buildings have disappeared for parking. The statue in front of Faneuil Hall is of Samuel Adams, by sculptor Anne Whitney.

A boy enjoys a nickel frank from a pushcart in 1937. The transaction took place at the corner of Hanover and Blackstone streets between the North End and Scollay Square. The eastern side of Blackstone Street was leveled in the 1950s for the ramps of the elevated Central Artery.

A pushcart vendor pauses at Quincy Market in 1937.

Scollay Square, shown here in the early 1940s, was a favorite nightspot for sailors from the nearby Charlestown Navy Yard. The neighborhood entertained them with its arcades, bars, burlesque clubs, photo studios, restaurants, and tattoo parlors. Scollay Square paid for its sins when urban renewal leveled it in the early 1960s.

War, Recovery, and Boston at a Cross-roads

(1940–1950s)

Captain Robert Morgan and the crew of the *Memphis Belle* ride singly in Army jeeps down Tremont Street in June 1943. The *Memphis Belle,* a Boeing B-17 Flying Fortress, became the first plane to complete its 25 bombing missions in World War II, and its crew escaped injury. Important symbols, the plane and crew were dispatched on a nationwide tour to support the war effort.

Fred Apt, newspaper vendor for the *Boston Traveler,* spreads the news of the end of the war in Europe on May 7, 1945, the day Germany surrendered. Americans celebrated V-E (Victory in Europe) Day the following day, on May 8, and then V-J Day on August 15, 1945, after Japan surrendered.

Two Boston heroes throw out the honorary first ball at Fenway Park in April 1946. Army Sergeant Charles MacGillivary (right) won the Medal of Honor for knocking out four German machine gun emplacements during the Battle of the Bulge. Navy Lieutenant John F. Kennedy, honored for rescuing a crewman when his PT-109 was sunk in the South Pacific, was elected president in 1960. Both now rest in Arlington National Cemetery in Virginia.

On September 21, 1948, at the corner of Blue Hill Avenue and Quincy Street, residents mingle in front of Katz Drugstore. Known as Cherry Valley, these blocks on the border between Dorchester and Roxbury were home to families from Nova Scotia and Jewish merchants. Neighbors bought day-old Whoopie Pies from Drake's Bakery factory or shopped at the Max Andrews delicatessen.

Construction began in 1939 on the main block of classrooms at Boston University; the completed building is shown here in 1948. The tower at the far end would be joined within a year by a twin, which anchors a second block. This Gothic-moderne rampart, designed by Cram and Ferguson, and Coolidge, Shepley, Bulfinch, and Abbott, began a new campus for a university that had previously been on Beacon Hill, downtown, and in Copley Square.

In the 1950s and 1960s, football surpassed baseball nationally as America's most popular sport, especially when professional football teamed up with television. But most football competitions took place on gridirons unnoticed by television. On October 28, 1950, a Dartmouth player tackles a Harvard player during a junior varsity game at Soldiers Field, next to Harvard Stadium.

On a February day in 1950, vintage autos had the honor of going first through the southbound tolls at the opening of the Mystic River Bridge. Connecting Charlestown and Chelsea, the bridge is a vital Route 1 link between Boston and the North Shore communities. In 1967, this cantilevered truss bridge was renamed for former Boston mayor and Massachusetts governor Maurice Tobin.

A policeman directs traffic at the corner of Dover and Harrison streets in 1952. Dover Street in the South End had been the heart of a crowded Jewish immigrant community early in the century. First-generation immigrant Mary Antin described Dover Street as simultaneously "a gate of paradise" and "prison" in her 1912 memoir, *The Promised Land.*

By contrast with streets overrun by automobile traffic, this unidentified Boston street corner, circa 1948, teems with women and children.

On this quiet Boston street on June 24, 1952, children play, mothers shop, and a few horse-drawn carts remain amid the automobiles.

Dwight D. Eisenhower rides in an open car down Blue Hill Avenue on November 3, 1952, the day before he was elected president. Republican candidate Eisenhower carried Massachusetts, over Democrat Adlai Stevenson, by 54 percent in 1952 and 59 percent in 1956.

This October 1956 view of Copley Square, from the New Old South Church, shows the second John Hancock building in the Back Bay, rising behind Trinity Church (Episcopal). Designed by Cram and Ferguson and completed in 1947, its pyramidal tower and weather beacon became a Boston landmark. In 1975, the third John Hancock—New England's tallest skyscraper—arose between Trinity Church and the Copley Plaza Hotel.

A new ramp of the Central Artery provides a vantage point for this June 29, 1956, view of Blackstone Street. Despite challenges, the Haymarket continues the traditions of four centuries of open-air produce market in downtown Boston. Photographer Leslie Jones may have wanted his photograph to show the Central Artery sweeping past old traditions, but 50 years later, the Central Artery is gone and Haymarket remains.

Notes on the Photographs

These notes, listed by page number, attempt to include all aspects known of the photographs. Each of the photographs is identified by the page number, a title or description, photographer and collection, archive, and call or box number when applicable. Although every attempt was made to collect all data, in some cases complete data may have been unavailable due to the age and condition of some of the photographs and records.

II BOSTON LIBRARY IN COPLEY SQUARE
Boston Public Library, Print Department
#46074

VI BOSTON AND LOWELL
Photo by Baldwin Coolidge
Boston Public Library, Print Department
#76620

X BOSTON AND PROVIDENCE
Boston Public Library, Print Department
#06277

3 CATHEDRAL OF THE HOLY CROSS
Boston Public Library, Print Department
#76681

4 LEWIS AND FULTON STREETS
Boston Public Library, Print Department
#30740

5 THE FRANKLIN STATUE
Boston Public Library, Print Department
#93995

6 OLD NATIONAL THEATRE
Boston Public Library, Print Department
#76503

7 OLD TORRENT 6
Photo by A. H. Folsom
Boston Public Library, Print Department
#76142

8 OLD SOUTH MEETING HOUSE
Boston Public Library, Print Department
#19050

9 OLD MASONIC TEMPLE
Boston Public Library, Print Department
#93874

10 FANEUIL HALL SQUARE
Boston Public Library, Print Department
#76059

11 USS KEARSARGE
Boston Public Library, Print Department
#53294

12 MASSACHUSETTS INSTITUTE OF TECHNOLOGY
Boston Public Library, Print Department
#32722

13 TEARING DOWN FORT HILL
Boston Public Library, Print Department
#06809

14 FRANKLIN STREET
Photo by James W. Black
Boston Public Library, Print Department
#76677

15 PEARL STREET
Boston Public Library, Print Department
#76617

16 CITY SQUARE
Photo by James W. Black
Boston Public Library, Print Department
#84397

17 WASHINGTON AND WARREN STREETS
Photo by Augustine H. Folsom
Boston Public Library, Print Department
#76141

18 CYCLORAMA BUILDING
Boston Public Library, Print Department
#76524

19 STATE STREET
Boston Public Library, Print Department
#76613

20 JOHN QUINCY ADAMS HOUSE
Boston Public Library, Print Department
#30752

21 BOYLSTON MARKET
Photo by Baldwin Coolidge
Boston Public Library, Print Department
#76493

22 SCOLLAY SQUARE
Boston Public Library, Print Department
#76990

23 WASHINGTON STREET
Boston Public Library, Print Department
#76343

24 **CHINESE FUNERAL**
Boston Public Library, Print
Department
#06673

25 **HARVARD COLLEGE
MEDICAL SCHOOL**
Boston Public Library, Print
Department
#29994

26 **TRINITY CHURCH**
Boston Public Library, Print
Department
#94290

27 **FANEUIL HALL**
Photo by Frank T. Layden
Boston Public Library, Print
Department
#06150

28 **THIRD BATTALION, BOSTON
LATIN SCHOOL**
Photo by Augustine H.
Folsom
Boston Public Library, Print
Department
#76166

29 **CORNER OF PRINCE AND
SALEM STREETS**
Boston Public Library, Print
Department
#96033

30 **TRIAL RUN OF SUBWAY CAR**
Boston Public Library, Print
Department
#23238

31 **TRIAL RUN FROM PARK
STREET STATION**
Boston Public Library, Print
Department
#76376

32 **COPLEY SQUARE**
Boston Public Library, Print
Department
#76267

34 **UNION OYSTER HOUSE**
Boston Public Library, Print
Department
#76240

35 **ST. PETER'S CHURCH**
Boston Public Library, Print
Department
#06040

36 **PARK SQUARE**
Boston Public Library, Print
Department
#76661

37 **POST OFFICE SQUARE**
Boston Public Library, Print
Department
#32509

38 **MERCHANT'S ROW**
Boston Public Library, Print
Department
#76060

39 **CASTLE SQUARE THEATRE**
Boston Public Library, Print
Department
#94279

40 **PARK STREET**
Boston Public Library, Print
Department
#89155

41 **TEMPLE PLACE**
Photo by Thomas E. Marr
Boston Public Library, Print
Department
#93915

42 **VIEW OF THE WEST END**
Boston Public Library, Print
Department
#76278

43 **UNION STATION**
Photo by Thomas E. Marr
Boston Public Library, Print
Department
#94386

44 **VICE-PRESIDENT THEODORE
ROOSEVELT**
Photo by Thomas E. Marr
Boston Public Library, Print
Department
#84480

45 **DEDICATION OF THE
GENERAL HOOK STATUE**
Boston Public Library, Print
Department
#76435

46 **PRINCE HENRY'S VISIT
TO THE STATE HOUSE**
Boston Public Library, Print
Department
#89008

47 **ENGINE ON
WASHINGTON STREET**
Photo by Thomas E. Marr
Boston Public Library, Print
Department
#77430

48 **LALLY BROTHERS**
Boston Public Library, Print
Department
#02412

49 **JIMMY COLLINS**
Photo by Edmunds E. Bond
Boston Public Library, Print
Department
#st10622

50 **CROWD ON THE FERRY**
Boston Public Library, Print
Department
#76247

51 **SHERWIN-WILLIAMS**
Boston Public Library, Print
Department
#06_01_000645

52 **SPRING STREET AND
POPLAR STREET**
Photo by Edmunds E. Bond
Boston Public Library, Print
Department
#02207

53 **WASHINGTON STREET**
Photo by Thomas E. Marr
Boston Public Library, Print
Department
#76581

54 **PAUL REVERE HOUSE**
Photo by Thomas E. Marr
Boston Public Library, Print
Department
#76829

55 **BOSTON PALACE CAR**
Boston Public Library, Print
Department
#77025

56 **SUFFOLK COUNTY
COURTHOUSE**
Photo by Leslie Jones
Boston Public Library, Print
Department
#05_01_000282

57 **SCOLLAY SQUARE**
Boston Public Library, Print
Department
#76987

58 **SLEIGHING ON BEACON
STREET**
Photo by Thomas E. Marr
Boston Public Library, Print
Department
#93920

59 **CHAMBERS AND SPRING
STREETS**
Boston Public Library, Print
Department
#53791

60 **HARVARD STADIUM**
Photo by Leslie Jones
Boston Public Library, Print
Department
#st11286

61 **HARVARD STADIUM FROM
THE AIR, AS IT USED TO BE**
Photo by Leslie Jones
Boston Public Library, Print
Department
#st10175

62 GRANITE WORKS
Photo by Leslie Jones
Boston Public Library, Print
Department
#06_01_000643

63 CORNER OF WESTLAND
AVENUE
Photo by Thomas E. Marr
Boston Public Library, Print
Department
#02062

64 BOWDOIN SQUARE BAPTIST
CHURCH
Boston Public Library, Print
Department
#89149

65 FIRST MASSACHUSETTS
MILITIA
Photo by Leslie Jones
Boston Public Library, Print
Department
#02190

66 BEACON HILL
Photo by Thomas E. Marr
Boston Public Library, Print
Department
#07199

67 INFANTILE PARALYSIS
Photo by Frank B. Conlin
Boston Public Library, Print
Department
#76444

68 MOLASSES DISASTER
Photo by Leslie Jones
Boston Public Library, Print
Department
#02143

69 COPLEY SQUARE
Photo by Leslie Jones
Boston Public Library, Print
Department
#02164

70 NORTHERN AVENUE BRIDGE
Photo by Leslie Jones
Boston Public Library, Print
Department
#02375

72 NEW SPRINKLING
DEVICE
Photo by Leslie Jones
Boston Public Library, Print
Department
#06_01_000628

73 READVILLE TRACK
Photo by Leslie Jones
Boston Public Library, Print
Department
#st10594

74 GOVERNOR COOLIDGE AND
BLACK JACK PERSHING
Photo by Leslie Jones
Boston Public Library, Print
Department
#89081

75 VIEW TOWARD DOCK
SQUARE AND NORTH END
Photo by Leslie Jones
Boston Public Library, Print
Department
#29615

76 HOTEL SOMERSET
Photo by Leon Abdalian
Boston Public Library, Print
Department
#02194

77 CHARLES PONZI
Photo by Leslie Jones
Boston Public Library, Print
Department
#02152

78 SOUTH BOSTON FISH PIER
Photo by Leslie Jones
Boston Public Library, Print
Department
#96060

79 FIRE ENGINE
Boston Public Library, Print
Department
#23346

80 M.S.P.C.A. FOUNTAIN
Photo by Leslie Jones
Boston Public Library, Print
Department
#29754

81 STUART STREET
Photo by Leslie Jones
Boston Public Library, Print
Department
#02326

82 FAN PIER
Boston Public Library, Print
Department
#29944

83 QUINCY MARKET
Boston Public Library, Print
Department
#06_01_000640

84 STUART STREET
Photo by Herald-Traveler
Boston Public Library, Print
Department
#84943

85 FANEUIL HALL AND QUINCY
MARKET
Photo by Leslie Jones
Boston Public Library, Print
Department
#06_01_000635

86 BUSY TREMONT STREET
Photo by Leslie Jones
Boston Public Library, Print
Department
#06_01_000625

87 AMELIA EARHART
Photo by Leslie Jones
Boston Public Library, Print
Department
#02026

88 ART ROSS, JR., AND
BENNY GRANT
Photo by Leslie Jones
Boston Public Library, Print
Department
#st10565

89 HAYMARKET SQUARE
RELIEF HOSPITAL
Photo by Leslie Jones
Boston Public Library, Print
Department
#07663

90 SPIRIT OF ST. LOUIS
Boston Public Library, Print
Department
06_01_000618

91 CUSTOM HOUSE TOWER
Photo by Leslie Jones
Boston Public Library, Print
Department
#06_01_000623

92 PASSENGER PLANE
Photo by Leslie Jones
Boston Public Library, Print
Department
#02122

93 NORTH STREET
Photo by Leslie Jones
Boston Public Library, Print
Department
#06810

94 UNITED SHOE
MACHINERY BUILDING
Photo by Leslie Jones
Boston Public Library, Print
Department

95 COPLEY SQUARE
Photo by Leslie Jones
Boston Public Library, Print
Department
#30360

96 NEIGHBORHOOD BOYS
Boston Public Library, Print
Department
#06_01_000620

97 PUSHCART RUSH
Photo by Leslie Jones
Boston Public Library, Print
Department
#06992

98 BATHING IN THE FROG
POND
Photo by Leslie Jones
Boston Public Library, Print
Department
#02654

99 **CITY HOSPITAL**
Photo by Leslie Jones
Boston Public Library, Print
Department
#84965

100 **SOUND TRUCK**
Boston Public Library, Print
Department
#76371

101 **GUAY'S BAKERY**
Photo by Leslie Jones
Boston Public Library, Print
Department
#02525

102 **MARKET DISTRICT**
Photo by Leslie Jones
Boston Public Library, Print
Department
#02033

103 **BIG BLIZZARD**
Photo by Leslie Jones
Boston Public Library, Print
Department
#89180

104 **THE USS CONSTITUTION**
Photo by Leslie Jones
Boston Public Library, Print
Department
#02174

105 **WOMEN'S NAVAL RESERVE**
Photo by Leslie Jones
Boston Public Library, Print
Department
#04991

106 **CAMPAIGN AGAINST
PROHIBITION**
Boston Public Library, Print
Department
#76163

107 **READVILLE RACE TRACK**
Photo by Leslie Jones
Boston Public Library, Print
Department
#st10466

108 **BUDWEISER**
Boston Public Library, Print
Department
#77040

109 **FRANKLIN DELANO
ROOSEVELT**
Photo by Leslie Jones
Boston Public Library, Print
Department
#02446

110 **RACE AT SUFFOLK
DOWNS**
Photo by Leslie Jones
Boston Public Library, Print
Department
st10592

111 **THE "NANTASKET"**
Photo by Leslie Jones
Boston Public Library, Print
Department
#06_01_000622

112 **JOHNNY KELLEY**
Photo by Leslie Jones
Boston Public Library, Print
Department
#02141

113 **CRADLE OF LIBERTY**
Photo by Leslie Jones
Boston Public Library, Print
Department
#06_01_000637

114 **HOT DOG STAND**
Photo by Leslie Jones
Boston Public Library, Print
Department
#06099

115 **VENDOR AND CART**
Photo by Leslie Jones
Boston Public Library, Print
Department
#53477

116 **WAR'S END**
Boston Public Library, Print
Department
#93715

118 **SCOLLAY SQUARE**
Photo by Leslie Jones
Boston Public Library, Print
Department
#06_01_000632

119 **"MEMPHIS BELLE" CREW**
Boston Public Library, Print
Department
#93721

120 **JOHN F. KENNEDY WITH
CHARLES A. MACGILLIVARY**
Boston Public Library, Print
Department
#77940

121 **BLUEHILL AVENUE AND
QUINCY STREET**
City of Boston Archives

122 **BOSTON UNIVERSITY**
City of Boston Archives

123 **GAME AT SOLDIERS FIELD**
Photo by Leslie Jones
Boston Public Library, Print
Department
#st10309

124 **DEDICATION OF THE MYSTIC
RIVER BRIDGE**
Photo by Arthur Hansen
Boston Public Library, Print
Department
#77752

125 **DOVER AND HARRISON**
City of Boston Archives

126 **CROSSING THE STREET**
City of Boston Archives

127 **STREET SCENE, 1952**
City of Boston Archives

128 **EISENHOWER IN BOSTON**
Photo by Leslie Jones
Boston Public Library, Print
Department
#02427

129 **COPLEY SQUARE**
Photo by Leslie Jones
Boston Public Library, Print
Department
#06_01_000624

130 **BLACKSTONE STREET**
Photo by Leslie Jones
Boston Public Library, Print
Department
#06_01_000636